CHAPEL PRAYERS

OF

George Rudolph Freeman

PROFESSOR OF HEBREW AND OLD TESTAMENT LITERATURE
MEADVILLE THEOLOGICAL SCHOOL

Published as a loving Memorial by his Students

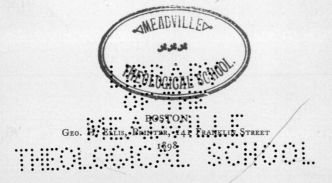

BOSTON
GEO. H. ELLIS, PRINTER, 141 FRANKLIN STREET
1898

PREFACE.

PRAYER may be either appeal, thanksgiving, or
aspiration,— one or all. He who in an assem-
bly guides the devotions of others is the judge of
what their needs and the circumstances of the hour
demand of him. While he speaks for himself, he
must also and still more speak for those who are
looking to him for the expression of that which lies
but half revealed in the silence of their own hearts.
With worthier conceptions of the divine nature and
deepening consciousness that God is not far away,
but that we are no nearer to ourselves than he to
us, appeal gives place to longing, and petition to
communion. Then our nobler thought of God no
longer allows us to pray, as did Israel of old, to the
" God of battles,"— Jehovah of hosts,— nor to him
that "sitteth upon the circle of the earth, and the
inhabitants thereof are as grasshoppers"; neither
in our thankfulness to the great Giver do we make
the empyrean ring with hallelujahs : rather, in the
silence, we listen to the "still, small voice."

The Chapel Prayers here gathered as a fitting
memorial of a beloved teacher by grateful disciples,
who were privileged to feel their inspiration as they
came fresh from his heart and lips, have realized
for them the poet's ideal of devout aspiration,—

"Prayer is the soul's sincere desire."

That transparent sincerity which characterized his
whole life shone out with special radiance in those
expressions of what he most wished both for himself
and for those who day by day were longing with
him to sound the fathomless "depths of God" and
to reach ideal heights of human endeavor. He
valued much that freedom from prescribed form
which the recognized liberty of the place allowed,
and which he felt to be the surest safeguard against
that devotional cant which always tends to smother
the healthy life of the spirit. Although he did not
realize that he had such a lofty mission, it can
hardly be doubted that these simple, earnest, and
truthful utterances of his had a permanent forma-
tive influence upon the minds of not a few who
needed just such a well of inspiration to save them
from spiritual drought. That intellectual upright-
ness which made the utterances of the lecture-room

a constant object-lesson in the noblest ethics became in the chapel-desk the glow of an equally pure and noble ethical purpose. He had no thought that these prayers would answer more than the immediate call of the hour of devotion which gave them birth, but none the less he deemed it a duty to clothe them in a worthy garb. Extemporaneous effusions of shallow feeling, dressed in stock phrases, gave him no joy. The duty pressed upon his conscience of ever giving his best in thought and speech to the service of the Highest. Thus have been saved for wider and more helpful use than he had planned those winged words of the morning, which else might have passed within the clouds of forgetfulness.

The necessary editorial supervision of the collection has been intrusted to her who, taking his name, grew into such intimate knowledge of his thought and shared so completely his whole life that to her alone this task belonged by right.

GEORGE L. CARY.

A SKETCH OF HIS LIFE.

GEORGE RUDOLPH FREEMAN was born Sept. 20, 1850, at Gettysburg, Penn. That he enjoyed a happy boyhood in the quiet of this prosperous farming country was evident by the keen pleasure he ever afterward felt and gave to others in rehearsing the memories of its mingled tasks and play. As his mental powers ripened, he was no longer content with the training of the country school-house; and his ambition carried him to the Lutheran College in Gettysburg. Here he won his earliest distinction as a strenuous and successful student, and on his graduation he was retained as an instructor in the preparatory department. With this occupation he combined a year's study in the Lutheran Theological School; but the craving for a richer culture drew him to the Graduate School in Yale, where he gave himself to the classics and modern languages. In this atmosphere, however, the clear, strong call of his nature to theological inquiry asserted its power, and, in order to provide means for the achievement of this purpose, he returned at the end of one year to the task of teaching. After two years in Gettysburg and one in Bethlehem, Penn., he began a distinguished career in the Yale Divinity School, which was crowned by the school's greatest honor, the Hooker Fellowship. At the end of his first year as resident Fellow in New Haven, he married Mary, daughter of Rev. P. B. Wilcox, of Northboro, Mass. For the ensuing two years he was in the University of Berlin, occupied especially with the critical study of the Old Testament under Professor August Dillmann. In the spring of 1888 he returned to America, and for six months served as the pastor of the Orthodox Congregational Church in Dexter, Me. The reconstruction of his theological views made him desire a more generous freedom of thought and a renewal of his critical inquiries. These conditions were made possible by his appointment to the Williams Fellowship in the Harvard Divinity School. In his first year at Cambridge he still preached occasionally in Congregational pulpits. In the second he was regularly engaged by the Unitarian parish in Wayland, Mass.

Most of his Unitarian preaching was done at

this time, although for a few years after removing to Meadville he still appeared with some frequency in the pulpit. Although himself a tireless seeker for the true form of conviction, Mr. Freeman aimed by his sermons to quicken and refine the aspirations and loyalties of Christian life and conduct rather than to discuss the questions and answers of Christian doctrine. A gentle, spiritual nobility, a certain tender sacredness of feeling and expression, gave a penetrating influence to his outwardly quiet discourse.

It was not, however, as a preacher that Mr. Freeman was to reach his full significance. The years thus enumerated were the preparation for a final and powerful activity in a theological professorship to which he was called in the Meadville Theological School in the year 1890. It was here that his abilities had their fullest play, but his success as a teacher did not rest upon the mere possession of intellectual talent. It was grounded in his whole character. His personality won the heart and mind of pupils and associates. The simple, direct naturalness of his manner, his kindliness and delicacy of feeling, a quick and careful thoughtfulness for others, while his uncalculating goodness

made him forgetful of self,— these traits made him
a valued friend in his work of teaching. The same
characteristics pervaded his intellectual life. The
learner found in him an acute and eager intelligence, a sympathetic understanding which clari-
fied and animated the great mass of his knowledge ;
but his extraordinary modesty and deference to
other men hid his power and attainments from himself. While this lack of self-recognition intensified
his labor over the drudgeries of minute details of
critical investigation, his strenuous persistency bore
rich fruit. He was constantly deepening and re-
fining his knowledge. It was the spectacle of an
organic and continuous intellectual life, faithful to
the slightest demands of the scientific conscience,
and yet grasping the leading points of view and con-
veying the result with a clear, delightful simplicity.
His humility and ardor gave saintliness to his
achievement of professional duty. Popular applause
might have been won by a fraction of the labor,
but the austerities and weariness of his work were
willingly endured in his devotion to a higher per-
fection.

His studiousness was not a thing apart from his
teaching. They were one and the same thing. He

labored to give. He conceived himself only as a teacher, and only reluctantly listened to urging that he should wrest from his too engrossing instruction some leisure to prepare his learning for a wider audience. The expansion of the programme of the Meadville School reflects the growth in range and the orderliness of method in his scientific scholarship. At the outset he had, besides his main department of Old Testament literature and comparative religions, accessory work in German and New Testament Greek. As he relinquished the latter to other hands, he added new courses in his proper field. The alternation of courses and the combination of classes allowed him to cover a large field of work. At the last he offered six courses on the Old Testament : —

1. Hebrew Literature, detailing the processes and results of the higher criticism.

2. The Religion of Israel, co-ordinating in an organic history the growth of religious ideas.

3. The History of Israel, a determination of political and social conditions.

4. The History of Messianic Ideas within the canon of the Old Testament.

5 and 6. Courses on the Minor Prophets and the Psalms.

In addition to the foregoing he gave an optional course in Hebrew, and to the Seniors a very learned and interesting study of comparative religions. In this last field he might have been expected to become before long a fruitful writer. Beginning at first, as was his wont, with points of view received from others, he came to conceive the subject in an independent scientific fashion, the presentation of which would have been of the greatest value. The appearance of his name on the prospectus of contributors to the new *Archiv für Religionswissenschaft* seemed to promise the activity for which his friends hoped. His literary publication was, however, limited to reviews contributed to the *New World*, the *American Historical Review*, the *Unitarian*, the *New Unity*. Before his last illness he had engaged to contribute an article to the *New World*, and he looked forward to a happy summer in this task, and in fresh studies of Semitic philology. The last two summers of his life were spent in Germany, where, with the stimulus of Professor Bernhard Stade's lectures, counsel and friendship, he had elaborated his materials for instruction.

It is the record of a rich, expanding life, which

set no near goal for itself, and carried the promise of large accomplishment in the future. We are not permitted to see the attainment of these results. A sudden and acute attack of illness found him exhausted from his long labors, and on the evening of Easter, April 10, 1898, after less than twenty-four hours of suffering, his earthly life came to an end.

FRANCIS A. CHRISTIE.

A TRIBUTE.

PROFESSOR FREEMAN'S scholarship may be characterized by the two words "fulness" and "caution." He was a wide reader, ransacking all sources for material in his chosen field, yet knowing how to give to each its due weight. He neglected no book, and he let none pass without sifting. His fine sense of proportion kept him free from crotchets and vagaries. Nature endowed him with good judgment; and this, by reading and reflection, he trained into critical soundness. His opinions on books relating to the Old Testament were valued because it was known that he was clear-headed, impartial, and impersonal. No man was ever less polemic than he; yet he none the less was able to indicate with distinctness the weak points of an hypothesis, and to oppose what he thought wrong, always, however, with such quietness and kindness as robbed opposition of its sting. This unbelligerent character of his critical work may often have escaped notice, but it must be regarded as a very important part of his scholarly outfit. It would be hard to exaggerate the harm that has been done Biblical research by the antagonistic temper of mind that has often controlled it,— a temper sharply opposed to fairness and insight. Not the least valuable of the legacies Professor Freeman has left his pupils and friends is the recollection of his spirit of calm, dispassionate inquiry. He was an investigator, not an advocate. He carried this spirit even into his treatment of the opinions of his teachers (to whom he always showed a beautiful devotion), never accepting conclusions without scrutiny, often in the form of a question suggesting a difficulty, and at the same time its solution. His genial intellectual hospitality was always accompanied by an equally genial *skepsis*. These qualities were apparent in him when he studied with me (rather as co-worker than as pupil) in the Harvard Divinity School, and they became more marked when he entered on his work as teacher at Meadville. This was his proper work. His happy combination of traits not often found together — large intelligence, frank recognition of authority, unfeigned modesty, and critical acumen and severity — made him an admirable guide for young men. It is a pity that the power of such a personality cannot be handed on, in complete form, from generation to generation, especially when the man leaves few written records of his work. What Professor Freeman wrote makes us regret that he did not write more. His caution in the formation of final judgments, and the high standard of performance which he held up before him, made him linger over his work. If he had carried out his literary designs, his writing, while marked by the breadth and sobriety that distinguished his thinking, would doubtless have shown less of a certain reserve which appears in some of his productions, — a reserve due simply to his unwillingness to commit himself to a position till he had examined it on every side.

CRAWFORD H. TOY.

HARVARD UNIVERSITY.

PRAYERS.

(*Sept. 29, 1892.*)

MAY we go forth to the duties of the day with willing hands and honest minds, with faith in the power of good over evil, willing to take our places in the mutual dependence of men and things; having that illumination which comes from moral conquest; believing in the saintship that compels life to be a paradise, that fashions heaven out of materials existing here and now; looking for no meed of blessing that we are not willing ourselves to bestow; expecting to be forgiven only as we forgive others; working and hoping for the day when the ties of human brotherhood shall hold in their strong embrace every otherwise isolated member of the human family, even as the tides of the sea embrace every broken reach of shore that opens its arms to receive.

And so may we each have a part in bringing upon the earth the kingdom of righteousness and of love. (Scripture Reading, Luke x. 25–37.)

(December, 1893.)

R EADY to take our places as dependent beings amid the solemn mysteries of our life, may we go forward to meet the experiences of the day. We would inquire diligently into all knowledge of a diviner life.

But we would not stand without as questioners only; we would enter; we would experience its seriousness; we would plead the cause of righteousness and of truth; with renewed confidence in great good yet unattained in our own and in others' lives, we would go on in doing our part to sweeten life, to invest it with a higher interest, to lift it into a purer atmosphere.

Thus, in a life of purity, of faith, of unconquerable love, would we rededicate ourselves, our knowledge, our experience, our work, to the ministry of healing and blessing the world. So would we place upon the altar of human need our myrrh and aloes,— the ministry of sincere, devoted, and unpretending lives. (Matt. xx. 20–28.)

(*April*, 1894.)

SPIRIT of love and truth and blessing, thou
who dwellest in the loving and upright heart,
we would walk to-day in thy fellowship. We would
yield ourselves readily to the voice within that
seems to be most divine. May there be ours that
illumination which comes from moral obedience,
and may there rest upon us in ever fuller measure
the blessing of moral conquest. One and another
worthy deed may we come to do with the ease of
instinctive action, walking among our duties and
meeting them as friends tried and old. We would be
humble in the presence of mysteries we cannot understand, and in the thought of truth we have not
attained ; but, encouraged by a growing confidence
in our better selves, we would surrender ourselves to
the dominion of the ideals that are calling us with
promise of point and purpose and potency to our
lives by redeeming us from our selfish selves, rais-
ing to a higher plane the life of every common day,
and making rare and beautiful all our interchange
of fellowship and thought. (Deut. xxx. 11–14 ;
Mark x. 37–42.)

I N communion with the divine life and in fellowship one with another, we would seek strength
and hope for a larger and more ready fulfilment of
the duties and obligations that devolve upon each
one of us.

As we come together each from his own tasks,
his own cares and anxieties, his own interests and
longings, we would unite in mutual fellowship, in
sympathetic thought ; and with reverent hearts we
would take each other's hands, and resolve that
care and grief and turmoil and temptation shall
have less dominion over us, and that the beauty
and strength and nobleness of life that have so long
been waiting to bless us shall now and henceforth
be granted their rightful place in our lives. So
would we rest in one another's love and sympathy ;
and in the stress and strain of life, its hope and its
doubt, its joy and its sorrow, we would find calm-
ness and comfort and rest for our hearts, and for
our minds peace and clear vision.

May the influence of our exalted moments rest
upon our souls with redeeming power, making clear
to us the relation between our visions and our
tasks ; and then, when duty and human need come

knocking at our hearts, may we obey the call, and so find the interpretation of our dreams.

So may there rest upon us that peace which is the cure of care, taking from love its anxiety, from bereavement its anguish, from desolateness its loneliness, resting upon human hearts as sunlight upon all the land this day.

(*Nov. 29, 1894, Thanksgiving Service.*)

INSPIRED and uplifted by this hour of common thanksgiving to thee, thou beneficent Source of the bounty and blessing that crown our lives, we would pray that this grateful and loving and helpful spirit may abide in our hearts and minds.

As we go to our homes, may the thoughts of the morning linger in our minds, and both gladden and inspire us. May we accept with more joyful hearts the simple blessings that supply our daily needs, the unnumbered comforts that minister to us on every hand, morning, noon, and night, rising up about us and beseeching us to let them bless us. O thou all-loving Spirit, we would rejoice more and be more glad in our homes, in the sweet converse there of kindred minds, in the love and peace that there enfold us.

Going forth from such homes to our daily duties, we would not forget the obligations that go with our heritage. We would be faithful in our duties and true to our responsibilities. Thankful for home and country, for our days of peace and for fellowship one with another, we would endeavor to fill out the measure of devotion of those who have gone before us by offering the service of earnest and faithful lives.

(*Jan.* 21, 1895.)

THOU divine Life, the Source of our own, and in whom we live, we would heed thy call to-day. Conscious of our own insufficiency, we would rejoice in the hope and help we have in thee. We would be glad in our sonship, and would accept the blessing and the health prepared for us from the beginning and waiting for us evermore. We have no words to call thee nearer or bring thee from the skies; but we would pray for that inward sincerity and earnestness and purity that shall make our vision clear, that we may see thee. We know that those who hunger and thirst after righteousness find the blessing and peace that attend a righteous

life. May that life with its blessing and peace be
ours !

May we listen to the call of the holy influences
that are always bending with their benediction over
us. Oh that we might open our souls to the wealth
of healing and redeeming power that is calling us
to peace and sonship with God ! Carrying with us
a confidence in the remedial power and possibilities
of every soul, of divine companionship and over-
brooding love, may we know how to interpret our
place amid the influences, the needs, and the duties
of the day. And with quick intelligence, with cheerful spirit, with the redeeming grace of charity, may
each fulfil this day's appointed tasks. Inspired
thus by a divine call, would we with loyal hearts live
the life that waits not to be ministered unto, but to
minister ; to it, with all its love, its peace, would
we devote our love, our thought, ourselves.

AS we recall anew our place in the universal
life, in the great unfolding of events,— as we
are reminded of the noble men and women of by-
gone years who lived and died in the faith of great
promises, having seen and greeted from afar the

things which have been fulfilled for us and are to
be fulfilled by us,— may we be gladdened and inspired,— gladdened at the thought of our heritage,
and inspired by the obligation that rests upon us to
perfect that which remains to be fulfilled. May
the simple grandeur of the Christ-life, and of the
faithful, trustful lives we can all remember, both
humble and exalt us. May we be high in our aims,
faithful in our duties, and true to our responsibilities, as were they in theirs ; and, though we cannot follow them in pursuit of high-appointed tasks
in undiscovered lands, may our spirits be ever rising to new and fresher heights along the steps by
which they mounted upward when they were here
among men.

By a life of sincere devotion to our highest ideals
of duty, to the most helpful life we know how to
live, may we both commemorate the past from
which we inherit so much, fill out the measure of
devotion of those who have gone before us, and do
our part in turn for the progress and well-being of
the world. So may we work with our might to
bring in the happier day, when the good shall
triumph, and the crowning race, the Christ that is
to be, shall reign.

And in this our choice of a life of love and service may all high and noble influences attend us with their light and their blessing, and thus may the life of each one of us grow to be more helpful and beautiful and loving. (Heb. xi. 40.)

(Good Friday, April 12, 1895.)

SPIRIT of life and truth and love, in communion with thee would we begin another day. May we be grateful for the hallowing and helpful influence of Jesus, and of all those who, like him, have spent their lives, not for selfish ends and aims, but for what they deemed the world's highest good, and then by their death have sanctified all that was noble and gracious in their lives. May we be so like them, may we so feel their fellowship with men, that they may become in our lives a redeeming power, drawing us away from all that is unworthy in thought and aim, and claiming us for every high aspiration and honest effort.

We would not forget that the price of our redemption has been precious, that on every side we are compassed by blessings that have been purchased for us through suffering and self-devotion

and self-sacrifice. We would not spend our days
and years in selfish enjoyment simply of that which
others have wrought out for us. Remembering that
the world is not yet fully redeemed, that the spirit
of brotherhood and self-renouncing love is the only
cure for its trouble and unrest, we, too, would join
the noble fellowship, and keep faith in our day
with these high principles, with this redeeming
love.

In all our life may the Christian spirit attend us,
keeping us in unswerving fidelity to every high
demand, in cheerfulness and sweet content through
the routine of humble duties and unexciting cares,
and in such sympathy and fellowship with those
who need that we shall be willing to take up our
cross and live for them. And so may the peace of
God which passeth understanding keep our hearts
and minds. (John xvii. 18–26; v. 9–19; vi. 2, 4–9,
16–20.)

(*February*, 1896.)

THOU divine Life, the setting of our own, pressing upon us on every side with ideals hal-
lowed by sincere souls in all time, we would be
quickened by thy fellowship. Reverently and lov-

ingly would we yield ourselves to each suggestion
of noble resolve, to every whisper of hope for a
better life, to all the silent ministries that are
urging us every day to fashion from our opportunities some more courageous and more helpful
career. We would discover anew this day in the
experiences of life some fresh possibilities of bet-
terment in our actual conditions, and would meet
the duties that devolve upon us willingly and
honestly. Thus may our lives be more than
echoes of that which men have attained in the
past in thought and in deed. To the thought we
inherit may we bring the enthusiasm of patient
study, of honest interpretation, and all we can of
added light. And may all our deeds one for
another be enriched by the personal interest of
large and loving hearts. And, while doing our best
in honest thought and loyal life, may we walk reverently and humbly in the presence of wide reaches
of duty not yet compassed, and of a nobleness of
life still unattained, meeting each morning with
new resolve, and finding each evening a larger
hope and deeper peace! (1 Kings viii. 22–24,
27–30; Isa. liv. 7–17.)

(November, 1897.)

SPIRIT of love and goodness, we would look up to thee in gratitude for the blessings that have crowned our days, and for the beautiful promises that are always calling us into the possession of better and nobler things.

May we be willing to follow thy call and to walk in the ways illumined by thy blessed light. We would pray that the duties of the day may appear to us not as so many burdens to be borne or as so many unattractive tasks to be hastily performed, but to be so related to our life one with another that in the doing of them we may be expressing our mutual interest and love.

And, while we enjoy the heritage wrought out for us by the faithful souls of all the past, may we remember that they, apart from us, cannot be made perfect; that we, too, owe a debt of service to the world.

We would be grateful for the high fellowship of thought we have one with another in our common pursuit of truth. We would seek together for that wisdom by the following of which we may all find blessing and health of soul. And so may there rest upon us that peace which abides with those

who are true to the best they know, and who hope
in God,— that peace which passeth understanding.
(Jer. vii. 1–7; Isa. xxxiii. 15, 16, 20–22, 24;
Hos. ii. 18–23.)

OVERBROODED by an intelligence greater than
our own, encompassed by a beauty and order
which human thought is powerless to approach, we
would rejoice in our heritage, and gladly open our
souls to the wealth of healing and redeeming
power. May there abide with us all that divine
love which no night can chill, no darkness deepen,
no calamity or separation quench. May we be led
by its gentle ministrations, O Spirit of light and of
love, and in all the joy of hearing our own names
called by thee may we know how to interpret our
place amid the needs and duties of life.

May we listen not only to thy voice, but may we
hear the voice of human need that comes calling
for our help. Carrying with us a sense of divine
companionship, may we meet the opportunity of
every day with increasing pleasure. Oh that we
might have in all our life, in every home, that
cheerful spirit, that generous sympathy, that beauty

of affection and of love, that exclude every jarring interest, every cold and withering word from which the misery of a life may come!

Inspired by the divine call offering blessings to ourselves, we would be awakened anew to the beauty and attractiveness of a life of loving service. We would live that life with all its love, with all its peace, with the sanctity with which it encircles every human soul, and be related by it here and now to "realms that know not earthly day." (Gen. i. 1; 1 John iv. 19.)

A S we stand before the mystery of our vision of God and of things divine, we would pray, O Spirit of light and of truth, that it may be granted us, not only to enjoy, but also to understand and to do; that we may not stand enraptured and bewildered by the divine glory, lost in our own delight, but may know how to find our visions translated by the needs of every common day.

The enthusiasm reached in high and rare moments, the ideals we thus come to have of our own possible selves and of what we might do to help others in the perplexing and anxious questions of their lives, may we be willing to trust and to endeavor to make real in the life about us.

Carrying with us a sense of divine companionship, conscious of our heritage from generations past, may we never stand bewildered between our visions and our tasks, but find in them and in every opportunity for human help the heavenly call to us to be artists in divine things, making real in human lives and institutions our visions and our ideals.

To the unseen Love which, we trust, is the heart of the world, in which we live and move and have our being, in which we confide as perfect in righteousness, justice, and tenderness, we would dedicate our work, our life, our love, ourselves. (Acts x. 1–19.)

SPIRIT of truth, of love, of helpfulness, and of peace, we would have thy fellowship and blessing to-day and always. We would ask that we may receive, seek that we may find, knock that there may be opened to us a knowledge of the truth, that we may learn how best to live, how to conduct ourselves on the upward and onward way into an evermore blessed and hopeful future.

May a divine discontent possess us, and may we seek to know the deepest, most serious truths of our life and all its mysterious meaning. An honest spirit we would have in dealing with ourselves and with others, and a constant adherence to truth in thought and in deed.

May we never palter with our convictions of what is right and true; but, by a whole-hearted and serious purpose, may we strive to find the truth about the life we are called to lead. And then, not satisfied with merely aspiring toward it, may we in all seriousness endeavor to live it.

In this our quest for truth we would not attempt to stand alone. We would be quickened by a sense of fellowship with serious and honest lives that have touched our own. May divine love rest upon all our souls. May it dwell in us, awakening in every life a holy and blessed harmony.

(Presentation of a flag to the public school, Monhegan Island, Me.)

ETERNAL Spirit, whom men worship under different names, and whom we have been taught to call our Father, we would rededicate ourselves to the cause of freedom. We would remember afresh with what a price our liberty has been purchased,— with what heroic devotion our forefathers maintained the sacred rights of independence, and how, within the memory of many of us here, fathers and sons, neighbors and friends, gave their lives in the struggle that set free millions of our fellow-men.

We would recall anew the heroic endeavor, the godlike devotion to the cause of humanity, which have made the past of our great country so brilliant and so glorious.

While we sing over again the patriotic songs sung so often by the heroes of the past, while our hearts swell and beat faster with unselfish emotion, we would reconsecrate ourselves to our country's highest good, to the end that it may never in our day, for want of our work, suffer from oppression or unjust laws; that we may give it to those who come after us, a habitation fit for free-born, independent, liberty-loving men and women.

As we unfurl to the free air this emblem of our country's institutions and laws, we would pray that, as it floats from year to year over this place of instruction, it may hallow the place with its sacred significance; that it may not seem to the boys and girls, the young men and maidens, who gather here as only so much material — so many stripes and clustered stars,— but as standing for liberty and independence, for justice and righteousness, for sympathy between man and man.

As they cross and recross this threshold, busy with their simple tasks and happy games, sharing the rich gladness of their golden days, may the meaning of their flag be diffused as an atmosphere about them, and thus become a part of the sweet, glad, beautiful hours of their school-day life. Breathing the atmosphere of freedom their flag suggests, may they grow toward independence of thought, from selfishness to unselfishness, being diligent in self-control in the homely round of daily duties, in the keeping of their word, too intelligent to be deceived by demagogues, too independent and self-respecting to be enslaved by either State or Church.

And, when the affairs of the nation come to devolve upon them, may they see to it that through no fault of theirs shall government by the people, for the people, and of the people, in their day fade from this fair land.

For us and for them, for to-day and for the days
to come, we put our trust in thee, in the confidence
that

"We cannot drift beyond thy love and care."

(*December*, 1897.)

O THOU divine Life and Spirit in whom our
lives are set and upon whom we depend, we
would turn to thee in gratitude for the blessings
and the opportunities that are pressing their in-
vitations upon us with each recurring day.

We would be grateful for the opportunities
granted us in these quiet retreats, so far removed
from the world and its cares, for study and for
communion with the great and good minds of the
world. We would pray that grace may be granted
us to be worthy of such high privilege. We would
not rest in ignoble ease, but would be stirred and
kindled by a noble discontent that shall urge us on
to ever greater endeavor and more divine achievement.

May we be unwilling to be receivers only amid
the blessings of the world, but may we strive to
give as well. And may the opportunities of each

day, its blessings, its privileges, even amid humblest duties and least interesting cares, rest upon our souls with redeeming power, summoning us to ever higher planes of noble and beneficent life.

Thus, undaunted by the vast reaches of divine living, in blessed fellowship one with another, may we go on rejoicing in the better way. (Hos. xiv.)

IN communion with the spirit of truth and of blessing and in fellowship with one another, we would seek light and help and courage in the experiences of our life. In the midst of perplexities that disturb us, of anxious cares that fret and worry us, of disappointments that are our daily food, of sorrows that weigh upon us, we would seek out all strengthening, helpful, and uplifting influences; we would rest our hearts upon them, and with all readiness take our places as dependent beings who are called to work out the mystery of life. With reverent hearts we would seek those influences in which is our strength, in which alone we can live our highest life.

We know that the humble and lowly in spirit are blessed, and do enter the kingdom of peace. May we be among them! We know that those who sin-

cerely mourn the evil of their lives, and henceforth turn their hearts and wills toward the right,
are comforted. May we, too, find comfort! We
would be pure in heart, so that we may see God.
May we be helped this hour and strengthened, not
only to see the way of peace and sonship with God,
but may our feet be led therein.

With eager, questioning, worshipful hearts may
we come thus to know the meaning of that new
birth of thought and will and purpose and feeling
which is being born from above. And thus may
doubt and darkness flee away, and may we walk in
the knowledge and the light of the new life. And
may we have the will and the wish, as light and
blessing come to ourselves, to help others to such
light and blessing. We would have faith in the
power of good over evil, trusting "that good shall
fall at last . . . to all, and every winter change to
spring." "And, growing in faith ourselves, may we
then reach out the hand of our own faith and
touch some other hand,— the hand of those in
doubt, of those in fear and darkness!"

Thus may there be put away from ourselves and
from all about us all that is evil, unkind, and un-
generous, and may we together reach out toward
all that is fair and just and good.

May peace and trust be with all who mourn for
loved ones gone away. Out of sorrow and pain
may there arise a blessedness and a hope whisper-
ing eternal comfort and peace. And, if our pathway must be strewn with disappointments and with
sorrow, may we not regret that love hath been, but
prefer our pain with the peace that is born of want,
and continue to hope and trust and love. (John
iii. 1–9; vii. 45–51; xix. 38, 39.)

CONSCIOUS of our heritage from the past, we
would take up the tasks of life with a renewed
sense of gratitude and of obligation. We would be
quickened by the thought of our fellowship with the
men and women of the past who have lived and
wrought for the best they knew. May we grow in
gratitude for the opportunities, the enjoyments, the
possibilities that are ours, because they have lived
and labored for us.

Reverently and lovingly would we treasure the
hallowing influences that linger upon us from the
lives of those with whom we have companied and
taken sweet counsel, but who walk and talk with us
now no more. May we not forget them,— those

sweet souls who were once our inspiration and our
strength! May they be our inspiration still, quick-
ening us each morning with new resolves and
blessing us each evening with brighter hopes. May

" Still their silent ministry within our hearts have place,
    As when on earth they walked with us, and met us face to
        face."

And though it may be hard to take up the burdens of life where they have laid them down, to
complete the task which they have left unfinished,
or to sing again the song which they have ceased
to sing, may there be granted us the needed
strength and courage to go on with renewed con-
secration in the pathway in which we have walked
with them. And so may we meet the opportunities
and duties of each day with a sense of the sacredness of life, discovering anew in our contact with
men and with thought the seriousness of living.

Inspired by the great cloud of witnesses by which
we are encompassed, and invited by calls of love
and duty, may we hope and work, and work and
hope, for the city of God, the new Jerusalem,
bounded not by walls of adamant or gates of pearl,
but wide and free as the hope and love and longing
and aspiration of human hearts!

(*March*, 1898.)

O THOU divine Life, in whose greatness the smallness and the fragmentariness of our imperfect lives may be taken up and blessed and forgiven and made more nearly complete, thou whose gentleness should make us great, we would be thankful for the beautiful promises that are always calling us to better and nobler lives.

May all that is dull and unreceptive of good in us be quickened and aroused to high devotion and holy will, that we may forever escape the dread coercion of evil deeds, the fatal unravelling of conscience, the days of feeble resolve, when the will would, but cannot, because it would not when it could. We would cultivate that holy zeal for righteousness of life, that constant resolution of soul, which will allow no opportunity to escape that might minister to a diviner manhood and to a larger service.

And may the thought that what we have sown that shall we also reap abide in our minds with all its fear and all its solemn joy. (Ezek. xviii. 1-5, 7-9, 19-32.)